Sonnets of the Soul

by Nancy E. Perry

Copyright © 2025 Nancy Perry

All rights reserved.

Everfield Press, Newberry, Florida 2025

ISBN: 978-1-946785-85-5

SONNETS OF THE SOUL

I dedicate this book to all those who have touched my heart.

CONTENTS

	Acknowledgements	p. v
	Introduction	p. vi - vii
1	**1956**	p. 8 - 11
2	**1970 - 1971**	p. 12 - 17
3	**1972**	p. 18 - 27
4	**1973 - 1974**	p. 28 - 35
5	**1975**	p. 36 - 43
6	**1976 - 1977**	p. 44 - 51
7	**1980, 1997**	p. 52 - 59
8	**before 2015**	p. 60 - 73
9	**2016 - 2017**	p. 74 - 83
10	**2024**	p. 84 - 89
	About the Author	p. 90

Acknowledgements

I would like to acknowledge the support of my daughter Karen Porter and Victoria Hill for shaping this work.

INTRODUCTION

This poetry book is a riveting account of experiences carried through Dr. Nancy Perry's life. These poems were written throughout Dr. Perry's life when she could really delve deeply into her personal experiences and process them in timely poetic ways. Some of the author's poetic descriptions were written from a point of view we can all historically relate to as the important events of her life unfold. Other poems were deeply personal about love lost and found. Millions of people have lived through the same history. Understanding the point of view of an individual's experience brings fresh light to our world. The author reveals their deeply held and treasured experiences of life with its poignant moments and all that can bring.

Sonnets of the Soul is the inside story of a life deeply and profoundly lived. A major focus in the poetry book is the suffering, loss, grief, love and passion experienced from the point of view of a psychologist, nurse, and artist. The author presents meaning related to her suffering, living, and passion that might help others.

1956

SONNETS OF THE SOUL

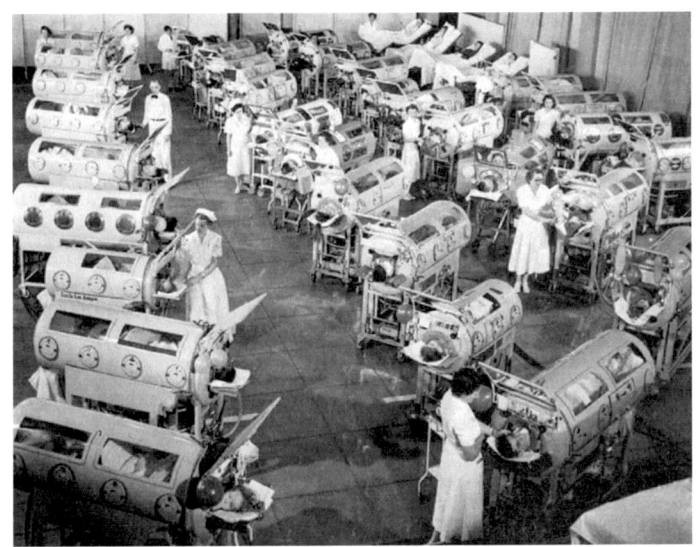

Iron Lung

Children in iron lungs during a polio outbreak at the Rancho Los Amigos Center in Los Angeles, California in the 1950s.

Photograph: Science History Images

1956 (22 years old)

The Last Polio Epidemic

Hiss and sigh a metallic tune,
Iron lungs beneath the moon.

Children trapped, a captive sight,
Gasping breaths, in darkest night.

Machines whirring, a sickening drone,
Tiny bodies frail and frightened,
Yearning for their mother's cheeks.

"Mommy", "Mommy", their desperate cries,
Echo through the darkened halls.

As I, a student nurse, stand vigil,
My heart is filled with unrequited grief.

SONNETS OF THE SOUL

1970 - 1971

SONNETS OF THE SOUL

Enlightenment
acrylic on canvas, 36 x 24

*Fall, 1970 Charbert's Coffee Shop, Columbus, Ohio
(36 years old)*

Mind Bending

Music is rocking…I listen.
Conversation comes from many roots,
Ideas like elements flow together.
Not blending…but setting off sparks in each other,
Changing often and rarely meeting with synergistic force,
Creating a new star never seen before.
I listen…I think…I care…

♦♦♦

Chabert's was a popular student hangout at Ohio State University. Graduate students would go there to discuss their dissertation ideas and work on their on their Ph.D.'s over coffee and baked goods. I was 36 years old and loved to listen to the discussions. I found the fusions of ideas to be an inspiration – an escape from the present and a door open to the possibilities of the future.

SONNETS OF THE SOUL

***Love**
acrylic on canvas, 20 x 16 inches*

Fall, 1971 (37 years old)

Love

Love is caring, acceptance of the faults and the beauty,
Love is tenderness and sensitivity to the other,
Love is nurturing and helps the other to feel strength and grow,
Love is trust and thrives on honesty.
Love is the complete revelation of mind, body, and soul to the other,
A sharing, mingling, touching.
Love can only be received as a gift.
Love needs to experience the other, to find openness, to know,
Love contains a commitment that says,
"I will always be there if you need me."
Love needs to touch and touch again,
To test and trust.
Love gives freely and demands nothing.
Love is to be cherished as the gift it is.
Love need not be returned in order to grow.

SONNETS OF THE SOUL

1972

SONNETS OF THE SOUL

SONNETS OF THE SOUL

Evolution
acrylic on canvas, 42 x 42 inches

1972 (38 years old)

Loneliness

The pain of loneliness,
Brought to bear upon separation.
The pain will go and other things,
Will fill the emptiness,
The quest goes on for meaning,
In human relationships.

SONNETS OF THE SOUL

Help! (Harvested)
acrylic on canvas, sketched in black and white

1972 (38 years old)

Reality

Reality crowds in through a barely opened door,
Casting light in unlikely corners of a room,
Kept shaded…lest it be discovered there.
Corners filled with an accumulation of dust and dirt,
Disturbed only by an occasional insect or piece of added trash.
The unwelcome light provides and awareness of a harsh reality,
Of unmet needs and growing discontent.
Perhaps a time of housecleaning is in order,
Or will that sparkling room be covered and the room darkened once more?

SONNETS OF THE SOUL

Dark Energy

26 x 34 inches, acrylic

1972 (38 years old)

Reserve

Giving, openness sharing, love.
If giving all and not returned,
What is left?
Must some be saved for another day?
Just in case…

Spirit
acrylic on canvas, 26 x 32 inches

1972 (38 years old)

Sensitivity

A new awareness, what to do?
Know thyself, they say:
Be in touch.
Feelings! Feelings! Feelings!
Joy, pain, love, hate,
Desire, yearning, excitement,
Feelings not allowed to surface,
Since childhood bring both joy and pain,
Guilt becomes a companion who smiles slightly
at the confusion.

SONNETS OF THE SOUL

1973 – 1974

SONNETS OF THE SOUL

Retribution
acrylic on canvas, 20 x 20 inches

Christmas, 1973 (39 years old)

Aftermath

Fires dampened, until only a few sparks remain,

Memories of a past luminescence linger like a pain.

The sparks may die or be rekindled again and again,

To brighten glories not known before.

SONNETS OF THE SOUL

Yearning
acrylic on canvas, 20 x 20 inches

Christmas, 1973 (39 years old)

Giving and Games

Why must love be sought after with games?

Must the gift of openness and trust be wasted,

By a response of manipulation and control?

Subtle tones of caring now gone from the response repertoire.

Replaced by chauvinism and double messages.

Can previous passions, openness, and trust ever be recovered from the ashes of this discontent?

One
acrylic on canvas, 40 x 30 inches

June 1974 (39 years old)

Confusion

Wanting, rejecting, loving, hating,
    Which is omnipotent today?
Values, decisions, wanting,
    Which for today?
Plan for the future, feel the "Here and now."
    Choose, choose, choose –
    Listen to head, feel with gut,
    Decide, decide, pick one.
These days there is dissonance,
    Appetites whetted; desires kindled –
What of others? Of right and wrong?
    They don't help me today.

SONNETS OF THE SOUL

1975

SONNETS OF THE SOUL

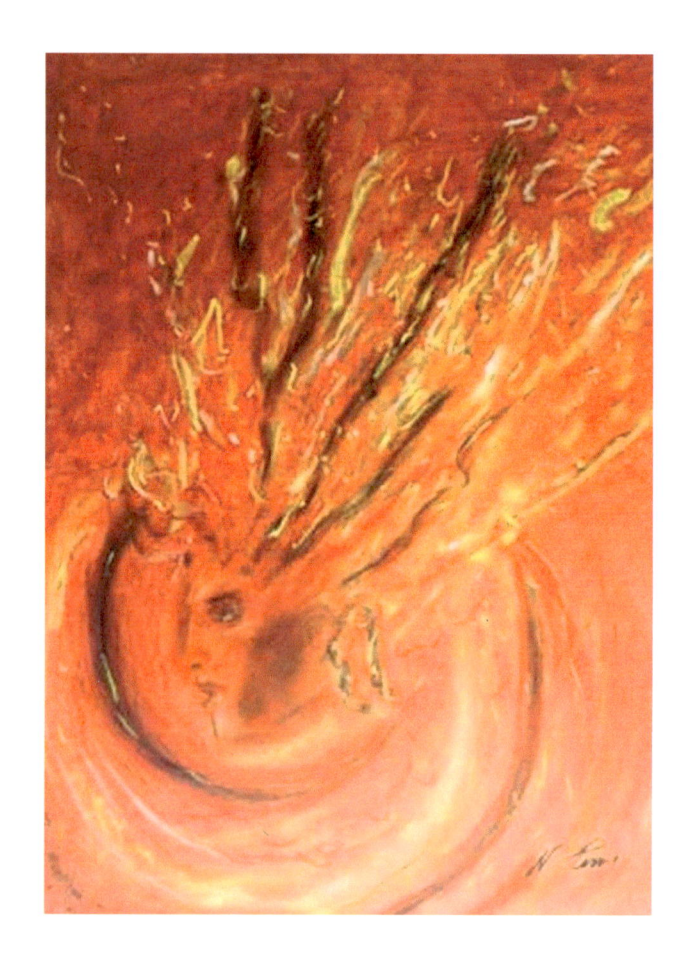

The Healer
acrylic on canvas, 20 x 16 inches

1974-1975 (40 years old)

Awareness

A new awareness… What to do?

Know thyself… They say,

"Be in touch."

Feelings! Feelings! Feelings!

Joy… Pain…. Love… Hate…

Desire… Yearning… Excitement…

Feelings not allowed to surface since childhood

Bring both joy and pain.

Guilt becomes a companion who smiles silently at the confusion.

Hope
acrylic on canvas, 20 x 24 inches

1975 (41 years old}

Potential

Thoughts of new, thoughts of old

The multitude of feelings –

The caring, the needing, the touching

The many loves of life –

The work, the play, the discovery

Life is filled with uncharted depths –

The exuberance, the elation, the revelation –

Awareness of beauty is beginning.

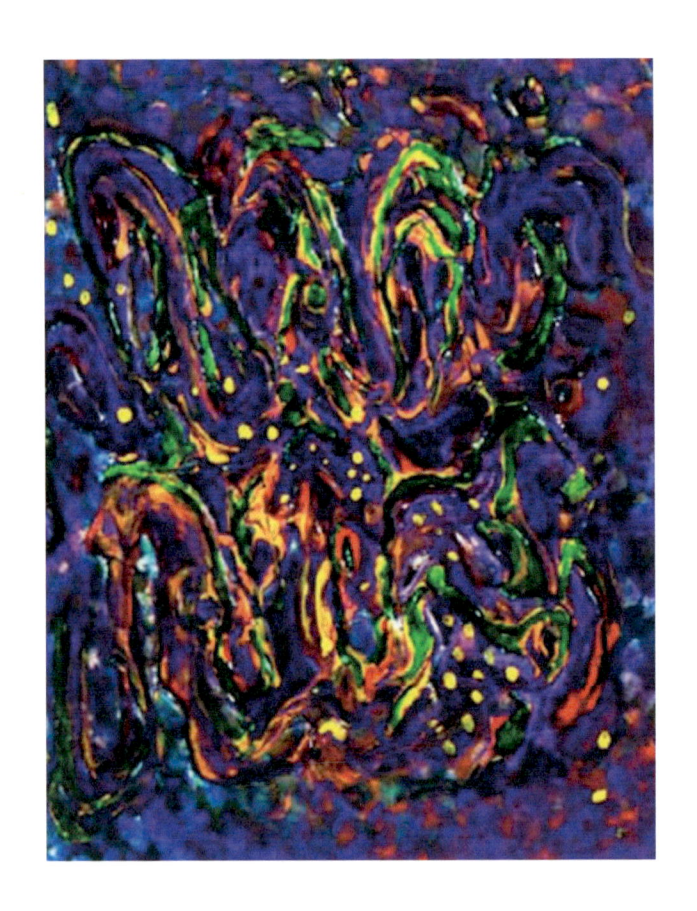

New Age
acrylic on canvas, 20 x 16 inches

July 17, 1975 (40 years old)

Respite

Time to think, time to dream,

Time to plan, time to wonder.

Fantasies burst forth in rapid succession,

Looked upon with interest and longing,

Feeling together now - What of tomorrow?

SONNETS OF THE SOUL

1976 – 1977

SONNETS OF THE SOUL

Man in Red

acrylic on canvas, 20 x 16 inches

December 1976 (42 years old)

Ode To a Blind Man

You constantly regaled me with descriptions of
trips we would take,
To places never seen before.
I didn't know you couldn't see.

Your beautiful gleaming car awaited, seemingly
well gassed,
Ready to take us to faraway places.
I didn't know you couldn't see.

Your vision, good enough for short forays on
well-trod paths,
To familiar places you'd been before.
I didn't know you couldn't see.

One day I asked to go with you, off the path to
new horizons,
You said, "Not now…wait…later perhaps…"
I didn't know you couldn't see.

You finally said "Alright," then got into your gleaming car,
Turned on the motor, and ran over me.
I didn't know you couldn't see.

As I lay on the ground, bleeding and near death, you looked at me,
You said "It's not my fault you know. You are responsible for the injury,
Because I am blind and cannot see."

♦♦♦

I wrote this poem while trying to decide whether or not to get a divorce.

SONNETS OF THE SOUL

Emerging
acrylic on canvas, 20 x 20 inches

12:30pm, Jan 1, 1977, to Bob (42 years old)

Goodbye

Goodbye my love,
Gone forever the warmth,
The looks exchanged that said "I know,"

Lost in the seas of life,
Forever…the passion, the trust.
The working together…the love,
Where did they go?

They were caught in the tide,
One day while I played in the sand.

(That was the day I built a most magnificent
sand castle.)
Good bye forever – my love.

♦♦♦

I wrote this poem the day I decided to file for divorce.

SONNETS OF THE SOUL

1980, 1997

SONNETS OF THE SOUL

Love
acrylic on canvas, 20 x 16 inches

September 1980 (45 years old)

Permission

What is happening?

Feelings of wellness coincide with memories of
the past
and stirrings toward future liaisons
I will not permit.

Memories of past loves with their tender
moments
and high adventure that takes one's breath away.
I will not permit.

Wondering thought about my lover and his
stirrings –
will he permit?

Opportunity rises like craggy rocks out of the
mist for him and me
I will not permit.

Growing older looms as an unknown forest that
must hold beauty and death,
I will not permit.

Fear of abandonment by my lover…like a stifled
cry
behind the eyes leads to momentary
panic…what then?

What of tomorrow? What of today?

The joy in his arms is more than enough…
but those stirrings…
I will not permit.

SONNETS OF THE SOUL

Intention
acrylic on canvas, 24 x 18 inches

12:00pm New Year's 1997 (62 years old)

Reclamation

Pulling my resources together,

Feeling my strengths,

Touching the weaknesses,

Exploring the pain.

Noting excitement, rebirth possibilities…

What will I be?

What will I do? Whom will I touch?

I feel the strength to move on,

To grow…to plan…to learn…to love…

SONNETS OF THE SOUL

before 2015

SONNETS OF THE SOUL

Metamorphosis

acrylic on canvas, 20 x 15 inches

SONNETS OF THE SOUL

2001 (67 years old)

To Jim

The sharing of heartstrings and secrets…of pain…of fun…of life,

the learning of art…of self…of thou.

To see the world through clearer eyes…the rescue,

Feeling the presence of your mind locked onto mine,

As I walked through the valley of the shadow of death,

Steadying me, guiding me, supporting me toward life and light,
Thank you.

Fragility
acrylic on canvas, 20 x 15 inches

SONNETS OF THE SOUL

before 2015
(from <u>Mother Bashing</u>, pg 49)

Alone

Alone on an island with you my love,
Feeling scared, can I do this?
And loving you so,

The twisting and turning, resenting and yearning,
So fearing, but freeing,
And loving you so,

The running and working, the feeding and playing,
But growing and learning,
And loving you so,

The teaching and hoping, the caring and coping,
With joy and commitment,
And loving you so,

We'll do it together forever and ever.
While loving you so.

The Wench
acrylic on canvas, 20 x 28

before 2015
(from <u>Mother Bashing</u>, pg 119)

Mother Knows Best

Now you know and then you don't,
Safe and serene, but then the leap.

Gone from sight the known way,
Like a ship that drifted out in the bay.

What is best and what is good,
To help you grow the best you could.

I need to learn all over again,
How to help and how to know,
My ways as mother, to teach you love.

Cosmos

Set of four, acrylic on canvas, 4 panels, 12 x 12 each

SONNETS OF THE SOUL

before 2015
(from <u>Mother Bashing</u>, pg 133)

Mother's Love

Mother's love,
Always there's a circle,

With my love just for you,
And then there appears a circle for two.

Sisters and brothers,
And neighbors and friends,

Experience the circle,
That grows and expands.

To envelop the earth,
With a love that's so pure,

It can pierce the darkness,
And light up the world.

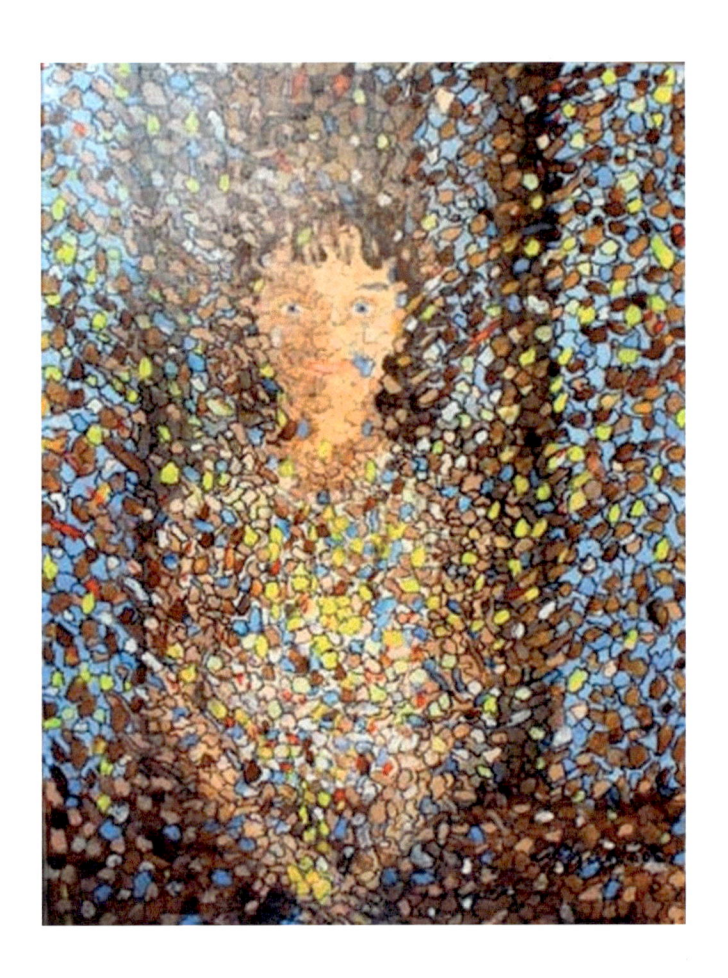

Self
Acrylic on canvas, 18x24

before 2015
(from <u>Mother Bashing</u>, pg 57)

Reality

Forgetting to remember and Remembering to forget,
Obfuscates the problem, to find the real truth.

Forgetting to remember and Remembering to forget,
Calms the fears and stops the tears,
But blocks the real truth.

Forgetting to remember and Remembering to forget,

Can hurt and harm or help confirm for what we yearn,
To believe our truth is real.

Swept Away
acrylic on canvas, 12 x 12

before 2015
(from <u>Mother Bashing</u>, pg 99)

Virtual Reality

I fly away to a faraway land,
A land free of pain,
A land of my choice and wildest imaginings.

To be who I want,
To get what I want,
To find love and excitement and freedom.

A land to learn ways to control,
It is the reality I want!
Is it real?

SONNETS OF THE SOUL

2016 - 2017

SONNETS OF THE SOUL

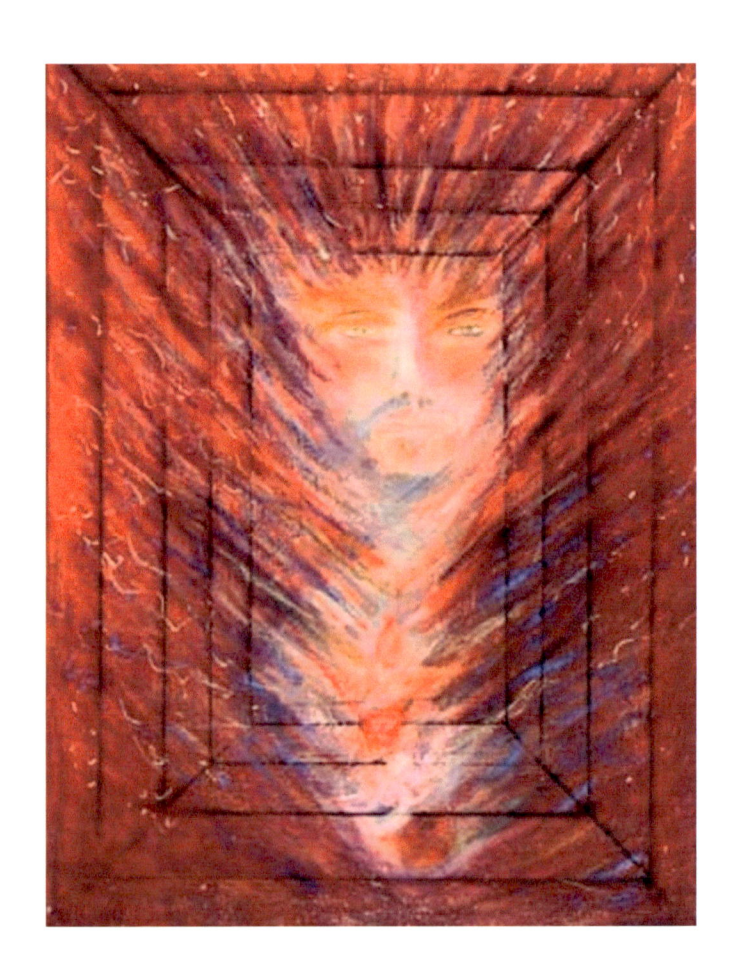

Guarded
acrylic on canvas, 24 x 18 inches

SONNETS OF THE SOUL

May, 2016 (after Dick died)

The Well-Armored Man

Dick was a well-armored man.

At first sight, I noticed a chink in his armor,
With only his eyes peeking through.
I learned very quickly that he cared about so many things.

I looked into those deep eyes and saw a soul so gentle,
My heart even skipped several beats.
His caring went deeply inside me and I sensed a resonance between us.

It was also very startling to notice that,
His eyes could see into me also.
The warmth in his heart often lit up his face,
And began to warm my heart too.

As time went by, his armor grew thinner,
I saw his integrity and honesty deep inside him.
His mind was often so busy thinking many

exciting thoughts,

Of robots, of science, of Star Trek, equality for all people,
And cars of all kinds.

Sometimes he shielded both of us with his armor,
When waters grew turbulent and ships were sinking all around.
He often used his armor as a safe and strong anchor,
I knew I was safe and felt peace in his arms.

As time kept on passing, this kind, soft-spoken man,
Gave me his heart, and I gave him mine.
Deep love continued to grow large between us,
Every day, every month, every year.
His armor around us became thinner and thinner,
Others now could even see in.
He felt joy in the seeing of others,
And allowed his armor to shrink.

There was much happiness in our seeing,
Life felt beautiful, expensive, and safe.
We knew each could truly see the other,
To be known and loved and accepted,
Became the greatest gift to us both.

Then one day I came home and soon learned,
My gentle and well-armored man had been called far away.
He had taken part of my heart away with him on the long trip that he had to take,
I was comforted as I knew that I still had part of his heart with me too.

To keep and to hold, and to cherish,
The communion of my soul with his soul,
Through our hearts that are connected forever,
Through time, and space, and dimensions.

However far away from each other we may be.

♦♦♦

This poem was written about my husband. Every morning, he would make me coffee and sing to me.

Freedom

September, 2017 (72 years old)

God Does Not Weep

God does not weep, only you do.
God does not judge, only you do.
God does not persecute, only you do.
God does not forgive, only you do.

God is the energy of love,
Within and around all living things.
Then, who must save this world?
The answer is, only you can.

SONNETS OF THE SOUL

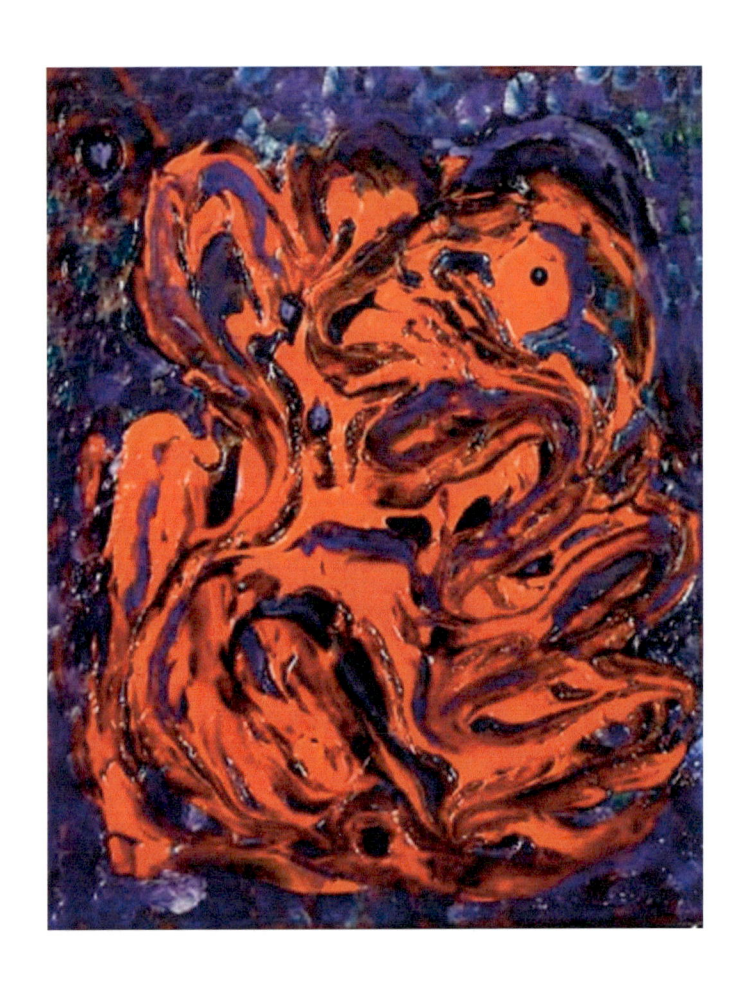

Center
acrylic on canvas, 20 x 15

2017 (83 years old)

You Touched Me

There's a place at my center,
Where the real me lives,
Away from superficial concerns:
Competition…pretense…social propriety…

It's a place where I'm alone with myself,
With all my joys…sorrows…cares…secret desires…
Sometimes it's a lonely place too,

When the realization comes that no one but me will ever know this place.
Sometimes the aloneness feels comfortable,
It's a place to be when the world becomes chaotic,

You came into that place one day…when I wasn't even looking,
And you touched me.

2024

SONNETS OF THE SOUL

The Mystic
acrylic on canvas, 20 x 28 inches

November, 2024 (90 years old)

What is Coming?

Muted footsteps approaching,

closer and closer.

What will happen when they arrive?

How to experience joy again?

Jumble

December 7th, 2024 (90 years old)

The Village

The village folk, a gathering bright,
embark upon our March toward Eternity.

With walkers, hearing aids, crutches, and canes,
We march together as a steadfast band.

With laughter shared, and stories told,
Our spirits soar, our hearts unfold,

As we savor life's delights each day .
We push our worries and doubts away.

When we must mourn our losses,
we often bid, a fond farewell,
to those who are called to continue their march
ever forward,
each to their own eternity.

ABOUT THE AUTHOR

Dr. Nancy E. Perry is a clinical psychologist as well as a registered nurse, author, and artist. She earned her Bachelor of Science in Nursing, and Master of Arts and Ph.D.'s in Psychology at Ohio State University. Her Associate Degree of Fine Arts was earned at Santa Fe Community College in New Mexico. Dr. Perry has served on the faculty of Ohio State University, the University of Wisconsin, and the Wisconsin Professional School of Psychology.

She is well recognized throughout the world for her work with trauma victims and dissociative disorders and has presented papers and workshops in many countries on these topics. Her last book was *Mother Bashing: Does She Deserve It?* Dr. Perry currently resides in Gainesville, Florida.

For more information about Dr. Perry's artwork visit:

drnancyperryauthor.com/paintings-gallery/

Made in the USA
Columbia, SC
05 April 2025

80c2d562-d344-46b8-86bb-e03a9b2ad84eR01